Old Man Oak

By: A J Crigler

Old Man Oak

Artwork and story by: A J Crigler
StoryTime Publications
P.O. Box 1644
Miamisburg, OH 45343-1644

Copyright © 2014 by AJ Crigler.

ISBN-13: 978-0615952680
ISBN-10: 0615952682

All rights reserved. No part of this book may be reproduced or transmitted in any form or by any means, electronic or mechanical, including photocopying, recording, or by any information storage and retrieval system, without permission in writing from the copyright owner.

This is a work of fiction. Names, characters, places and incidents either are the product of the author's imagination or are used fictitiously, and any resemblance to any actual persons, living or dead, events, or locales is entirely coincidental.

This book was printed in the United States of America.

To order additional copies of this book, contact: AJ Crigler at

www.ajcstorytimepubllications.com
email: ajcstorytimepublications@aol.com

Old Man Oak
By: A J Crigler

There is an old oak tree

in the middle of the yard.

Standing there for years

like a mighty faithful guard.

Sometimes it looks like a wrinkled old man,

all bent over with a cane in one hand.

The squirrels gather acorns

from off the tree and ground.

When the leaves fall in autumn

old oak makes a crackling sound.

He is covered in a blanket,

in winter after it snows.

I feel sorry for the tree

when the cold wind blows.

The wind starts gusting

like a huge fan.

Winter is never kind

to that poor old man.

He shivers and shakes,

quivers and quakes

and parts fall off

like big corn flakes.

Then spring comes and

melts the snow again

and things turn green

and the chirps begin.

Birds love to sit on

the branches in the shade.

Making homes in springtime

in nests that they have made.

In summer the oak stands tall

reaching towards the sky.

The sun warms old man oak

and makes him a healthy young guy.

The End

Old Man Oak

    Old man oak (OMO) is a story about an old oak tree that resembled a old man, which came from a poem I wrote. I woke up with the idea for the ***Old Man*** poem and the story developed from there. Most of my stories come from dreams or I wake up with the idea. In writing *OMO* it took 3 hours to write the poem. It is a story for children 6-12 and also some adults.

    Writing and illustrating ***Old Man Oak*** was challenging. It was exciting to develop pictures to go with the poem. It is a fictional fantasy and I hope everyone will enjoy ***Old Man Oak*** as much as I have creating it.

    Reading is essential to life.

Story Time Publications

www.ingramcontent.com/pod-product-compliance
Lightning Source LLC
Chambersburg PA
CBHW042119040426
42449CB00002B/107